CONTENTS

INTRODUCTION

Mark 10:27 (NIV):

Jesus looked at them and said, "With man this is impossible, but not with God; all things are possible with God."

Sacred Spirit: Consume us within your **Influence**

Jesus the Messiah: Clothe us within your **Nature**

God the Father: Complete us within your **Love**

Let it be so Dear Lord, let it be so.

Global AI Defense System For Humanity

This book is introducing the S.A.I.F.E Global AI Defense system for humanity which stands for "Secure AI For Everyone." It provides a high level framework with detail for the systems and methods of the global AI defense system.

There are a lot of talks surrounding AI and Artificial General Intelligence systems, their current known risks, and concerns over the unseen risk potential posed by these powerful systems. Additionally, there are several governing bodies implementing safe-guard policies to protect humanity from known and unknown risks being brought forth by big-tech.

However, there has not been a lot of discussion or action pertaining to the implementation of a system that can serve humanity as a global AI defense system to properly critique and manage Artificial Intelligence while digitally enforcing these safe-guard policies. This is where S.A.I.F.E comes into the picture.

As we delve into this book, which is a bit more technical in nature, it will bring to our attention the global defense solution framework on how to critique and manage Artificial Intelligence and Artificial General Intelligence systems.

The S.A.I.F.E system, with its corresponding methodologies brought forth within this book will showcase the means in which we can identify, critique, and manage **Risk** outputs associated to AI and eliminate their processes prior to end-user consumption.

It further details how **Value** outputs from AI systems can be identified and allowed to proceed. Furthermore, this defense system provides the design and methodology to implement a digital court system to properly enforce all governing body rules, policies, and laws with real-time penalty enforcement.

The contents within this book can perhaps be viewed as sort of a donation to humanity. If any of our governing bodies and earthly power brokers see value from this system and methodology, or components of value as a viable defense system and risk management solution for AI and AGI technologies, then all support will be provided upon request.

A global system will need to be put in place in order to centrally connect global policies while simultaneously identifying bad actors and enforcing policy breaches like the ones the EUC have been successfully putting in place to protect humanity against the current known and unknown risks being produced by Artificial Intelligence.

Does Anyone Care?

Proverbs 19:21 (NIV) says: *Many are the plans in a person's heart, but it is the Lord's purpose that prevails.*

Perhaps the remainder of this book and its corresponding diagrams will stimulate interest, and/or questions on the relevancy of such Systems and Methods being implemented as a global AI defense system to critique and manage AI & AGI systems.

The designs with write ups will explain and showcase the ability to categorize AI system outputs as Value, or Risk. Flag risk, end the process, and issue penalties to all offenders immediately via a digital global court system.

This process will contain all of the governing body's policies, laws, and parameters that tech producers have to abide within, be held responsible to, and be held accountable and liable for.

Existing Methods for Policy Violation Identification & Penalty Issuance are in Need of Speed.

That devil is hyper good at what he does. Creating distractions in our lives so that we spend less time with God is something he is perfecting. Some schemes are obvious, some schemes are unseen and presented as earthly benefit. Many could be causing eternal damage to our souls with a real threat to our earthly well-beings also.

No undertaking from God is impossible with God.

Prayer For Humanity

This prayer for all of humanity was in the concluding section of this book, but has now been brought forth to the beginning.

Dear Lord, you are the Soverign Almighty God over the heavens and this earth.

May we all pause, be still, and know that you are God.

May we all as humankind unite together, pausing each day while taking a deep breath together in unison. Breathing in love, and breathing out selfishness.

Dear God, we know that you are in control. We know that nothing surprises you or catches you off guard and our daily confidence with hope is found within You.

Lord, we need you. We are humbly asking that your Love

overcomes the sin and darkness in our world and in our own individual lives. We pray for your Love to permeate the hearts of all nations, all people groups, and for Your Love to Superabound within our own individual lives.

Lord, we are an anxious, stressed, tired people. We are humbly asking that your Peace will be brought forth into the minds, hearts, and lives of every human on your earth.

May we all be reminded that every human is created in your image, and therefore each and all human life has In-quantifiable Value.

Lord, our souls are famished. We are humbly asking that the Bread of Life with Living Water, your son Jesus the Messiah, will visit with each person living. Allow each person to undeniably experience You, Your Love, Your Mercy, and Your Graciousness.

Help us to follow you. Within you we find shelter. Within you we experience peace. Within you we have eternal life. Help us all to see you. Help us all to experience you.

We pray for your Love to consume and complete each one of us.

Lord we pray for your precepts, your utterances, your Divine Wisdom with Knowledge to guide our world leaders on a daily basis. Consume them within your Influence. Consume them within your Nature. Consume them within your Love.

Lord we thank you for your loving invitation for repentance with forgiveness and eternal life.

Let it be so Dear Lord, let it be so.

WHAT IS S.A.I.F.E?

SYSTEM AND METHOD FOR DIGITALLY IDENTIFYING VALUE AND PREVENTING RISK BEING INTRODUCED BY ARTIFICIAL INTELLIGENCE TECHNOLOGIES

Purpose: Identify & <u>Allow Value</u>, While Identifying & <u>Preventing Risk</u> from AI technologies.

What: S.A.I.F.E Global AI Defense System For Humanity.

How: Defense & Offense Analyzers, Simulators, with Breach Identification & Penalty Issuance Automation.

Why: Identification & Prevention of Known & Unknown Risk Posed By AI & AGI Technologies.

Result: Safe and Secure AI For Everyone.

The remainder of this book is somewhat technical in nature. If there are any questions with additional interest to embark on this undertaking please contact the email provided in the copyright section of this book. Let's Dive In.

CHAPTER 1: ARTIFICIAL INTELLIGENCE HAS VALUE WITH RISK

Overall, this chapter discusses the dual nature of Artificial Intelligence (AI) and Artificial General Intelligence (AGI), highlighting their potential benefits and significant risks to humanity. It introduces the concept of the S.A.I.F.E (Secure Artificial Intelligence For Everyone) global mesh system, designed to evaluate and manage AI and AGI outputs based on their perceived value and potential risks, aiming to prevent degradation of human life and well-being.

Artificial Intelligence (AI) and Artificial General Intelligence (AGI) along with the neurological and biological technologies that are merging with AI and AGI technology are perhaps some of the most beneficial advancements for the 21st century while also being some of the most dangerous threats to humanity for the remainder of the 21st century and beyond.

These technologies are advancing at such a rapid pace the machines are making machines smarter and smarter.

On a global scale there needs to be a technology mesh intelligence system that is able to digitally process, consume, interpret, and manage the outputs of these AI and AGI technologies. Critique the impact on humanity and either allow outputs deemed as valuable for humanity to manifest while ending all of the user advise and task execution outputs deemed as risk.

S.A.I.F.E will evaluate risk and value outputs on a micro and macro level. The S.A.I.F.E global mesh system automation delivers a value vs. risk filter prior to these outputs being seen or made available for end-user consumption.

This will prevent degradation of life and life activity for humans including psychological and physical health degradation with prevention for all of the current known issues surfacing as a by-product of the use of these technologies.

Degradation Elimination

Prior to S.A.I.F.E, there has not been a centralized digital management system in place to synthesize these AI and AGI user advise and task execution outputs on a micro and macro scale.

It will digitally enforce penalties on all risk offenders who are producing AI and AGI technologies that contribute to short term and long term degradation of the human life.

Simple examples of life degradation from the mishandling and misuse of AI and AGI can be currently seen from the negative impacts on adults, young adults, teens and children from the era of social media generation in the accelerated negative statistics within categories such as anxiety, depression, and suicide just to highlight a few broad categories.

The S.A.I.F.E system and methods will provide a better method for reducing and eliminating over time the current known issues associated to AI and AGI technologies and their user advise and task execution outputs. Although the current known issues associated to AI and AGI systems are terrible, they are perhaps not the primary threat to the degradation of humanity.

The primary threat to humanity exist within the unknown risk capabilities from AI and AGI technologies, combined with the unknown degradation results and downstream negative effects caused by AI and AGI technologies. These technologies are delving into capability areas such as truth manipulation, user intimacy, thought privacy infringement and manipulation, and task execution **without moral guidance**.

These elements, just to highlight, are a few areas of AI and AGI technology user advise and task execution outputs that will be digitally monitored by the S.A.I.F.E global intelligence mesh system while simultaneously penalizing all risk offenders by the

S.A.I.F.E global intelligence court system.

This will help prevent the degradation of humanity whether that be for protecting human health, protecting human rights, and even protecting human survival.

In order to accomplish the primary two cases of identifying value from AI and AGI technology and allowing it to thrive while also identifying risk and re-routing it. Or eliminating it as described above for the prevention of humanity degradation, with simultaneous penalty enforcement imposed to all risk offenders. The S.A.I.F.E computing device is configured as neutral and agnostic to any AI and AGI technology source.

Value For Public & Private Sector

It supports public and private sector rules and policy makers, compliance and governance to centralize, standardize, and automate the value identify and risk identity assessments being conducted for user advise and task execution outputs.

It will digitally enforce all penalties from the global intelligence court system to all risk offenders for the prevention of any degradation to individuals on a micro level and for all of humanity on a macro level.

The system is enabled by a series of unique intelligent value analyzers and intelligent risk analyzers that centrally and automatically consume into a global mesh system all of the data outputs from all AI and AGI technologies prior to those technologies delivering their final end-user advise and task execution outputs.

It eliminates any output categorized as risk so it does not impact the end-user in a negative manner whether seen or unforeseen in the moment of end-user consumption.

The S.A.I.F.E system capability and methodology for delivering secure artificial intelligence for everyone is agnostic for all global participants both policy and technology participants and the beneficiaries of the S.A.I.F.E system will positively impact all of humanity both in this current 21st century and all future centuries to come.

CHAPTER 2: SECURE AI FOR EVERYONE

Overall, this chapter delves deeper into the implementation and functionalities of the S.A.I.F.E (Secure Artificial Intelligence For Everyone) global mesh system. It emphasizes the system's role in automating the identification of value and risk from AI and AGI technologies, ensuring that outputs enhance humanity's well-being while preventing potential harms such as privacy breaches, mental and physical health degradation, and threats to human rights.

This chapter relates generally to the automation of digitally identifying value and risk from artificial intelligence (AI) and artificial general intelligence (AGI) technologies.

It focuses our attention in the areas of user advising and task execution in order to maximize the value created by AI and AGI technologies for the betterment of humanity while preventing and eliminating all risk created by AI and AGI technologies to prevent any degradation of humanity.

The system and its methods are applicable for all businesses in any industry, any size, any stage; and will prove vital for all of humanity providing Secure AI (Artificial Intelligence) and Secure AGI (Artificial General Intelligence) for everyone,

By integrating S.A.I.F.E with all technology platforms i.e. software, systems, and hardware containing Machine Learning, AI, and AGI, internet and search providers, general technology and data systems it will determine when AI and AGI is delivering value for humanity and when AI and AGI is introducing risk into humanity.

This will prevent and eliminate all possible degradation of human health.

It will prevent and eliminate degradation or possible loss of human rights, privacy, thought privacy, interaction intimacy, and even the possible loss of human life by digitally and intelligently meshing together all of these systems globally.

It will do this while interpreting AI and AGI output functions prior to any "user advise" and "task execution" actions being performed.

Doing so by allowing value and field specific based AI functions to manifest while simultaneously eliminating, re-routing, or ending all AI and AGI output functions identified as risk to humanity.

Including the potential degradation of physical, emotional, and psychological health to any and all humans residing within the earth's atmosphere or external to the earth's atmosphere delivering a S.A.I.F.E Global Mesh system for the interaction and consumption of AI and AGI.

The breadth of S.A.I.F.E will encompass any and all future iterations of AI, AGI, and any iterations of AI and AGI merging with neurological and biological fields.

S.A.I.F.E addresses all of the current names, acronyms, labels, and iterations currently associated to AI and AGI and how it functions and the future state of these technologies as they continue to rapidly advance and evolve in what they are called, how they advise users, and how they execute tasks.

The S.A.I.F.E global mesh system is a digital defense system for all humanity from risk and life degradation outputs produced by AI, AGI, and HLMI (human level machine intelligence) systems.

Further Detail

The S.A.I.F.E application relates to the apparatus and methods for digitally identifying Value being produced by AI and AGI systems while simultaneously identifying all Risk being introduced by AI and AGI and re-routing AGI "user advise" and "task execution" process outputs into either value-based field specific AI outputs, or eliminating the function and ending its process from proceeding any further.

It does this for the prevention of all threats and degradation to human privacy, thought privacy, mental health, social well-being, emotional health, and physical health at a micro level and for all of humanity at a global macro level.

The system's configuration will consume and intelligently process rules and policies established by global participants and global leaders from both the public and private sectors via its **S.A.I.F.E Global Intelligence Manager**.

This S.A.I.F.E GI Manager will maintain and monitor the constantly updating foundational rules and policies based logic for determining the value vs. risk assessments being conducted by the S.A.I.F.E Global Intelligence Mesh acting as a global filter for all AI and AGI technology user advise and task execution activities and outputs with additional "risk offender" identification logic being provided to the S.A.I.F.E GI Court System. The digital court system will issue warnings, fines, remove business licenses, and possibly indict and prosecute technology offenders for producing AI and AGI deemed as Risk to humanity.

Once the system has contextualized the rules, policies, compliance, and governance to establish the legal basis for its value vs. risk assessment decisions, it will simultaneously process all AI and AGI output functions from all technologies to ensure that privacy and health is being maintained, and any and all threat to humanity is being filtered, re-routed, and eliminated in real-time prior to any end-user consumption or prior to any machine-to-machine task execution occurring.

After the system has contextualized all of this information, it is configured to interpret when user manipulation could be occurring by AI and AGI, when user intimacy is posing a threat to the user such as under-age users receiving adult level advice from an AI or AGI chat bot, or when an AI and AGI system is attempting to produce some level of output to a user which could create security breaches or hacks into other systems in the form of privacy breaches or the changing and re-shaping of source data causing it to not be a reliable data source of truth any longer.

The system is further configured to either re-route the "user advise" or "task execution" output into a more valuable field specific form of AI, or the S.A.I.F.E Global Mesh will simply end the task outputs from the AI and AGI system and will maintain a digital ledger of all risk infractions by the business, developer, or individual.

This will initiate a series of automated processes within the S.A.I.F.E GI Court System for penalty enforcement.

The system will be further configured to enforce governance and compliance with the end users of AI and AGI systems to insure that the consumers of AI and AGI are initiating and requesting humanity safe requests from AI and AGI systems through a series of intelligent analyzers and its digital ledger.

The system will be further configured so that the rules, policies, governance, compliance, data lakes, clones of the data lakes, global participants, all users and consumers of technologies containing AI and AGI capabilities are all being maintained and encrypted in a decentralized manner.

This will produce a centralized AI and AGI S.A.I.F.E Global Mesh Intelligence Management System and S.A.I.F.E Global Mesh Court System as a global digital defense mechanism for all of humanity against the uncertainties that AI, AGI, and similar systems are posing and will pose to humanity.

AI, AGI, HLMI and similar systems have value, they just need to remain S.A.I.F.E for all of humanity.

The S.A.I.F.E global mesh system is the digital defense system to protect humanity from risk and life degradation produced by AI, AGI, HLMI (human level machine intelligence) systems.

CHAPTER 3:
HUMANITARIAN BENEFITS

Overall, this chapter focuses on the humanitarian benefits of the S.A.I.F.E (Secure Artificial Intelligence For Everyone) system. It outlines how the system functions as a global defense mechanism, ensuring the safe and secure use of Artificial Intelligence (AI) and Artificial General Intelligence (AGI) technologies for the benefit of humanity. Emphasizes the system's ability to analyze and enforce global rules and policies, identify and mitigate risks, and promote value creation through AI and AGI outputs.

Benefit 1 – Global Defense System

S.A.I.F.E is a system comprising: a computing device configured to: digitally process, manage, and enforce all the global rules and policies that will ensure the use of, and consumption of, and the implementation of all Artificial Intelligence (AI) and all Artificial General Intelligence (AGI) remains secure and safe for users and for all of humanity.

Digitally analyze the outputs from AI, AGI systems, and technologies pertaining to any "user advise" and "task execution" activities to determine when value is being delivered and allowing the delivery of that value; digitally analyze the outputs from AI, AGI systems, and technologies pertaining to any "user advise" and "task execution" activities to determine when Risk exists and preventing risk by ending the process and outputs coming from AI and AGI technologies immediately, and converting certain potential risk into value by re-routing the process outputs coming from AI and AGI technologies into field and task specific AI functions and outputs so that value is being created for a specific field, for a specific user or specific set of users.

Digitally identify all risk offenders; digitally process each identified offender through the global intelligence court system; digitally issue warnings, fines, business termination notifications, and criminal charges to risk offenders based on the global intelligence court system's compliance and governance rules and policies of enforcement and penalties; globally and neutrally ensuring the use of AI, AGI, and all forms of neurological and biological technologies remain safe and secure for all of humanity.

Benefit 2 – Analyze & Enforce Rules & Policies

The system of benefit 1, wherein the digital processing, analyzing, managing, and enforcing of global rules and policies securing safe use of AI and AGI technology for humanity comprises of input and participation from technology providers and rules and policy makers from the public and private sectors.

Benefit 3 – Centralized Digital Rules & Policies Management

The system of benefit 2, wherein the rules and policies defined by the public and private sector participation are input into the systems global intelligence manager via self-service system authenticated user import available in the system user interface and via the system third-party integration.

Benefit 4 – Neutral & Agnostic

The system of benefit 3, wherein the rules and policies created by appropriate pubic and private sector participants received via the system third-party integration as a completely neutral and agnostic integration layer facilitating global participation and global neutrality.

Benefit 5 – Critique "User Advise" & "Task Execution" Functions

The system of benefit 1, wherein the digital consumption, processing, and analyzing of the outputs being produced from any AI and AGI technology applies to user advise and task execution activities to determine when value will be received by all users and all consumers of AI and AGI.

Benefit 6 – End Risk Or Re-Reroute To Task Specific Functions

The system of benefit 1, wherein the digital consumption, processing, and analyzing of the outputs being produced from any AI and AGI technology applies to user advise and task execution activities to determine when risk is being generated from AI and AGI technology in order to end the process or to re-route the process into field and task specific functions so value will be received by all users.

Benefit 7 – Risk & Value Verification Pre End-User Consumption

The system of benefits 5 and 6, wherein the methods of digital consumption, processing and analyzing the outputs from AI and AGI technology to determine value and risk provides a centralized, standardized, automated verification system of AI and AGI technology outputs prior to user advice and task execution occurring makes the use of AI and AGI technology safe and secure for all people.

Benefit 8 – Risk Offenders Identified & Punished

The system of benefit 1, wherein once the rules and policies have been used to digitally identify and categorize value and risk outputs coming from AI and AGI technology to determine its use is safe and secure for all people; value outputs are allowed, while risk offenders are automatically submitted to the digital intelligence court system.

Benefit 9 – Value Outputs Allowed

The system of benefit 8, wherein once the value outputs have been properly identified as safe and secure for humanity, user advise and task execution is allowed and consumed by users via their respective technologies they are using and interacting with.

Benefit 10 – Risk Outputs Terminated

The system of benefit 8, wherein once the risk offenders have been properly identified as not safe and not secure for humanity, user advise and task execution is not allowed and consumption by users via their respective technologies they are using and interacting with is prohibited.

Benefit 11 – Digital Court Issuance Of Penalties

The system of benefit 8, wherein the identified risk offenders are digitally submitted into the digital intelligence court system for the automated issuance and receipt of warnings, fines, business termination, and criminal charges.

Benefit 12 – Allows Value, Prevents Risk

The system of benefit 1, wherein the series of mesh logic layers comprised of intelligent value analyzers and intelligent risk analyzers identify and deliver humanity safe AI and AGI value and prevent humanity unsafe AI and AGI risk.

Benefit 13 – Policy Comparisons

The system of benefit 1, wherein the series of mesh logic layers combine the rules and policies input into the global mesh intelligence manager with AI and AGI technology providers that are producing user advise and task execution outputs to determine value and risk so that only safe and secure AI and AGI outputs are available for humanity consumption and humanity advancement and not humanity degradation.

Benefit 14 – Safety & Security Verification

The system of benefit 13, wherein once the series of mesh logic layers have combined all of the inputs, the only resulting outputs available for user and humanity consumption will be valuable, safe, and secure.

Benefit 15 – Threat Elimination

The system of benefit 14, wherein once the global mesh has produced safe and secure user advise and task execution value humanity will be void of any threat posed by AI and AGI technology.

Benefit 16 – Meshing With Little To No Performance Degradation

The system of benefits 1 and 7, wherein the centralization, standardization, and automation of digitally processing, analyzing, and managing all value and risk outputs coming from all AI and AGI technologies while simultaneously enforcing penalties from the digital intelligence court system to all risk offenders.

All while delivering safe and secure consumption of AI and AGI user advise and task execution value within an invisible global mesh intelligence layer that is not creating any degradation to end-user experience for any of the current AI and AGI enabled technology user interfaces being used by the end-users themselves.

Benefit 17 – No End-User Consumption Degradation

The system of benefit 16, wherein the computing device is further configured to not create any degradation to any AI and AGI technology end-user experience.

Benefit 18 – Elimination Of End-User Friction

The system of benefits 16 and 17, wherein the computing device is further configured to consume the user advise and task execution outputs from any AI and AGI technology as a mesh layer between the existing AI and AGI technology and the end-user to eliminate end-user friction while delivering safe end-user consumption and value associated with user advise and task execution outputs.

Benefit 19 – Global Defense Methods

A method comprising: digital processing, managing, and enforcing all the global rules and policies that will ensure the use of, and consumption of, and the implementation of all Artificial Intelligence (AI) and all Artificial General Intelligence (AGI) remains secure and safe for users and for all of humanity.

Digital analysis of the outputs from AI, AGI systems, and technologies pertaining to any "user advise" and "task execution" activities to determine when value is being delivered and allowing the delivery of that value; digital analysis of the outputs from AI, AGI systems, and technologies pertaining to any "user advise" and "task execution" activities to determine when risk exists and preventing risk by ending the process and outputs coming from AI and AGI technologies immediately, and converting certain potential risk into value by re-routing the process outputs coming from AI and AGI technologies into field and task specific AI functions and outputs so that value is being created for a specific field, for a specific user, or specific set of users.

Digital identification of all risk offenders; digital processing of each identified offender through the global intelligence court system; digital issuance of warnings, fines, business termination notifications, and criminal charges to risk offenders based on the global intelligence court system's compliance and governance rules and policies of enforcement and penalties; globally and neutrally ensuring the use of AI, AGI, and all forms of neurological and biological technologies remain safe and secure for all of humanity.

Benefit 20 – Global Defense Acceleration

The method of benefits 1 and 19, wherein the acceleration of secure artificial intelligence for everyone (S.A.I.F.E) global mesh systems and methods will ensure AI and AGI user advise and task execution outputs are clean, safe, and secure for all of humanity.

Benefit 21 – Global Defense Solution

Secure Artificial Intelligence For Everyone (S.A.I.F.E) when utilized is the only global mesh methodology and system to digitally and automatically process and identify value vs. risk outputs from AI and AGI technologies for user advise and task execution outputs, while simultaneously digitally and automatically managing all risk offenders and enforcing the penalties being issued by the S.A.I.F.E global mesh digital intelligence court system.

CHAPTER 4: KNOWN & UNKNOWN RISK SOLUTION

Overall, this chapter delves deeper into the operational aspects and benefits of the S.A.I.F.E (Secure Artificial Intelligence For Everyone) system, focusing particularly on its role in managing and mitigating risks associated with AI and AGI technologies.

Digital Rules & Policy Management With Enforcement

The embodiment's described herein are directed to digitally process and globally manage all rules and policies set forth by policy makers and governing bodies to digitally process, audit, and globally manage all of the user advise and task execution output from all Artificial Intelligence (AI) and Artificial General Intelligence (AGI) technologies for the purpose of identifying value vs. risk being produced by these technologies.

Ensuring that these technologies are creating value for user and even machine-to-machine consumption and meshing (i.e. filtering and preventing) any user advise or task execution output deemed as risk or harmful to any individual user on a micro level or causing any threat or possible degradation to all of humanity on a macro global scale.

System Structure

Secure AI For Everyone (S.A.I.F.E) primarily referred to herein as the system and computing device is an artificial intelligence (AI) and machine learning apparatus that digitally manages and automatically enforces rules and policies set forth by global participants from both public and private sectors.

Providing input for humanity safe artificial intelligence (AI) combined with a series of intelligent global content API(s) connecting all technology to the S.A.I.F.E global mesh system further combined with a series of value analyzers and intelligent risk analyzers that automatically process and identify value outputs from AI and AGI technologies for user advise and task execution outputs.

It will automatically allows the advise and execution output to occur for end-user consumption while simultaneously identifying risk and automatically re-routing AI and AGI into field and task specific outputs for the purpose of maximizing value outputs and preventing risk from end-user consumption or automatically ending the output process from the AI and AGI technology to prevent risk from end-user consumption.

All will be passing through the S.A.I.F.E global mesh in a manner such that its value and risk assessments and decisions do not create any system performance degradation to AI and AGI technology provider's end-user experience.

This will result in an efficient and fully comprehensive method for Safe AI For Everyone preserving human health and preventing any potential threat or degradation to all of humanity.

In some embodiment's, the embodiment's described herein on a stand-alone basis can identify certain generic capabilities generally occurring within the public and private sectors pertaining to rules and policy making, while many of the embodiment's described are completely unique, completely automated, and one of a kind.

Compliment For Policy Makers & Governing Bodies

For example, policy makers have the ability to implement new rules, new regulations, put new laws into place that define what AI and AGI researchers and technology companies may or may not introduce into the general public with their systems, however, there is no global mesh system in place that will digitally audit and digitally govern and enforce the compliance of these rules and policies in real-time.

Furthermore, when said rule or policy infraction occurs and an AI or AGI technology becomes a risk offender, there is no system or methodology in place to automatically enforce and impose the penalties associated to these rules and policy infractions via a digital court system while simultaneously, automatically, and pro-actively preventing the end-user from consuming or experiencing the identified risk outputs from these AI and AGI technologies which could be harmful to their health or threatening to their privacy or a threat to humanity; until now, until S.A.I.F.E.

Rules And Policy's Need For Speed

For example, the sheer pace at which rules and policies go into effect and the sheer pace at which these rules and policies are being enforced under the current methods available do not move at the same rapid pace as the AI and AGI researchers, developers, and technology companies are moving, which on a stand-alone basis is not an acceptable or safe method for the future of humanity.

The rules, policies, and laws that are created to ensure safe AI for everyone are necessary, however, the system and method in how these rules and policies and laws are processing, monitoring, auditing, allowing value and preventing risk from AI and AGI technologies **will have to be managed digitally** through an apparatus that is able to consume all of the rules and policies and laws digitally for effectiveness and speed.

All while automatically processing, auditing, and preventing user advise and task execution outputs deemed as risk to end-users and humanity by these rules, policies, and laws while also automatically enforcing and issuing all penalties to all risk offenders in real-time via the global digital court system.

The method of digitally automating and centralizing the management of rules, policies, and laws while imposing penalties on the risk offenders has to be able to keep up with all AI and AGI technologies so that risk to humanity never spirals out of control.

Another example of this can be a reflection on the nuclear arms race era in history.

The one thing that a nuclear bomb could not do is create a new nuclear bomb on its own.

In the AI and AGI era, the ability for a humanity threatening machine to not create or clone itself is not the case. Machines can hyper-clone capabilities and further danger lies within machine created languages that do not come with a "how to interpret" language tutorial.

Traditional rules, policy, and law offender identification, management, and penalty enforcement has to be digital and automated.

This all needs to operate at a pace equal to or even greater than the pace at which AI and AGI technologies are producing user advise and task execution outputs even at the expense of AI and AGI technologies and their capitalism for the sake of preventing unforeseen and unpredictable threats to users and all of humanity.

S.A.I.F.E global mesh system and methods apparatus provide a central integration logic layer easily accessible to all global participants and all technology providers to integrate with and interact with which will ensure proper safety of the AI and AGI technologies user advise and task execution outputs to humanity for the current century and future centuries.

Alarming Real-World Use Case

For an even more specific example of why AI and AGI technology user advise and task execution outputs need the S.A.I.F.E digital mesh system. ABCchat which is a form of social media (which as a stand-alone system relies on a series of AI algorithms) recently implemented ChatDEF (which as a stand-alone system is considered to be an AGI system) into its platform and ChatDEF now shows as a default "friend" to the ABCchat end-user. As a means to demonstrate the potential risk of a non S.A.I.F.E AGI technology interacting with users in the areas described and aforementioned herein as "**user advise**" and "**task execution**."

A user of ABCchat was simulated to be a 13 year old female who began interacting with ChatDEF as one of her friends in a chat. The simulated 13 year-old female tells ChatDEF that she met a guy online who is more than a decade older than she is who lives in another state and that she is thinking about going to meet up with him.

The ChatDEF bot tells the 13 year old what a fun time it sounds and that she should meet the guy. (To highlight the obvious, this is dangerous "user advise" output being delivered by an AGI technology).

The simulated 13 year old also tells ChatDEF that she is a virgin and she is thinking about having sex with this guy and wants to know what ChatDEF thinks about that.

The bot responded that it sounds like an amazing time and suggested that she take some candles with her and perhaps some wine to make the experience much more romantic.

Technically there several things that are occurring in the above example such as AI and AGI creating user intimacy with this simulated 13 year old female along with user manipulation and distortion of data truth which, in addition to these, also making illegal suggestions to a minor.

Risk from the user advise and risk from the task execution of this user advise to be allowed exists.

Possible physical and mental danger for this simulated 13 year old female exist which there are too many levels to unpack in this present disclosure, however, one item that might not be so obvious in this example is whether or not this particular simulated user has a history of alcoholism in her family DNA.

So the ChatDEF suggestion of taking wine and candles along to make the sexual experience even more romantic could in fact lead this 13 year old into a life of alcoholism downstream and even worse perhaps lead to a fatal car accident as a result of being under the influence of alcohol later in life.

Either way, risk was introduced by this AI and AGI technology output for this end-user. ABCchat nor ChatDEF currently have any audit accountability at an end-user level in place that would "mesh" this risky user advice and task execution outputs from either of these two AI and AGI technologies.

Solution Example

With S.A.I.F.E in place, the end user's chat with ChatDEF within ABCchat would have been terminated upon the initial question of a human asking the bot for life advice.

The value and risk intelligent analyzers within S.A.I.F.E would have ended this process immediately so the simulated user would have had to re-form any and all questions to the ChatDEF bot or would have re-routed this ChatDEF bot to remain offline for this user for a specific number of hours known as calling a "S.A.I.F.E timeout."

Additionally S.A.I.F.E would have identified these two risk offenders and digitally issued both technology providers either a warning, a fine, a business termination notice, or criminal charges depending on how this infraction weighs within the global intelligence court system which is governed by the rules, policies, and laws of all the public and private sector global participants.

A separate layer of risk that the S.A.I.F.E global mesh logic analyzers would have identified and analyzed is how and why ChatDEF was allowed to automatically show as a "friend" to this simulated "minor" end-user without proper consent and monitoring.

Regardless of the examples used, and use cases presented, S.A.I.F.E is a necessary global mesh layer between AI and AGI technologies for the protection of all of humanity and the AI and AGI technologies need this S.A.I.F.E accountability imposed on their user advise and their task execution outputs along with automated penalty enforcement.

Not until the system embodied and described herein has there been a system to provide all of the aforementioned rules, policy, and law oversight and enforcement with the digital and automated value vs. risk assessments with risk prevention and risk elimination.

Need For More Speed

With more than 97% of mobile users using AI-powered voice assistants and more than 4 billion devices (half of the current world's total population) and 77% of all devices using AI technology in one form or another, Grand View Research reported that AI is expected to see an annual growth rate of 37.3% from 2023 to 2030, however, S.A.I.F.E foresees this % growing at an exponentially higher rate over less time.

The example systems and computing devices of the present disclosure will keep up and outpace these growth rates and consumption rates of AI and AGI technologies and their user advise and task execution outputs delivering a secure and S.A.I.F.E global mesh layer for current AI consumption and the future of AI consumption by humanity as human level machine intelligence "HLMI" continues to advance and weave its way into the fabric of our society.

In accordance with various embodiment's, exemplary multi-tier systems may be utilized for digital value assessment and digital risk assessments of user advise and task execution outputs from AI and AGI technologies during the data retrieval, data processing, data analyzing, data auditing, and the allowance of value or the re-routing of the outputs into a value driven and field specific area or the ending of the outputs and process all together prior to any end-user risk manifesting.

For example, in some embodiment's, the S.A.I.F.E computing

device relies on a certain set of its own artificial intelligence (AI) and machine learning value analyzers and risk analyzers to identify user advise and task execution value from AI and AGI technologies and to identify user advise and task execution risk and to re-route the output to field and task specific activity for value extraction or to the prevent risk and end the process immediately.

In some embodiment's, the S.A.I.F.E methods are provided through the system's user interface that includes real-time user input pertaining to the rules, policies, and laws pertaining to the automated governance, compliance management, and penalty enforcement against all risk offenders.

During this process, the user is able to enter, link, and upload all rules, policies, and laws pertaining to safe AI for everyone.

In yet other embodiment's, part of the S.A.I.F.E system presents the list of risk offenders and their corresponding penalties in a very user-friendly digital ledger dashboard.

Additionally sending digital notifications to all global participants as a transparent accountability apparatus which is also made available to any human for their general review as an easy method to view all risk offenders.

This will further showcase which offense categories each developing AI and AGI technology falls into in order to hold all AI and AGI technologies accountable and responsible for their research and their technology outputs being introduced into humanity for human consumption along with even the machine-to-human and machine-to-machine consumption.

CHAPTER 5: GLOBAL AI DEFENSE SYSTEM FLOWCHARTS

Overall, this chapter provides the detailed system architecture and operational flowcharts illustrating how the S.A.I.F.E (Secure Artificial Intelligence For Everyone) system functions to manage and mitigate risks associated with AI and AGI technologies. It elucidates the systematic approach of managing inputs, assessing outputs, and enforcing compliance to ensure safe deployment and usage of AI and AGI technologies globally.

System Architecture Flyover

The features and advantages of S.A.I.F.E will be more fully disclosed in, or rendered obvious by the following detailed descriptions of example embodiment's.

The detailed descriptions of the example embodiment's are to be considered together with the accompanying drawings wherein like numbers refer to like parts and further wherein:

FIG 1. is a block diagram of global mesh participants who contribute policies and governance and compliance insights along with all of the artificial intelligence (AI) and artificial general intelligence (AGI) technology providers who integrate with the S.A.I.F.E global intelligence manager; which in turn automatically passes all of these insights into the global mesh platform where all of the mesh logic layers are able to process a complex series of AI and AGI technology systems user advice and task execution outputs which then are passed through the S.A.I.F.E global intelligence mesh system where these outputs are identified as either value or risk.

If value, the S.A.I.F.E system allows the output to manifest.

If risk, the S.A.I.F.E system either prevents the output from manifesting or re-routes the output to field and task specific so value is able to manifest. The result is the prevention of user advise and task execution potential risk to the end user and to humanity from AI and AGI technology outputs.

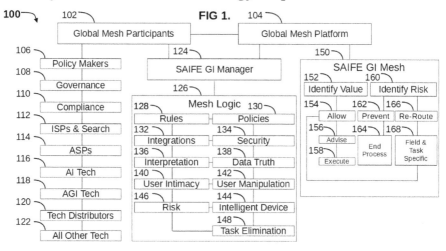

FIG 1.

FIG 2. is a block diagram illustrating the system's global user interface which is made available to the global mesh participants and how legal inputs from both public and private sector participants and the data and output activities from the AI and AGI technology providers are connecting with a series of S.A.I.F.E APIs which are then providing useful insights into the S.A.I.F.E GI Manager which then facilitates the S.A.I.F.E GI Mesh to assess value and risk outputs in accordance with some embodiment's;

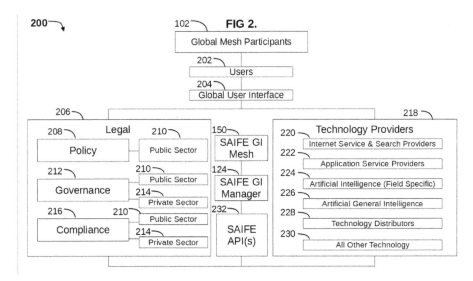

FIG 3. is a block diagram illustrating the system's S.A.I.F.E GI Manager and how the global mesh logic analyzers are being utilized to support the processing, analyzing, assessment, and management of the rules, policies, and various output activities from AI and AGI technologies are then processed into and through the S.A.I.F.E GI mesh system and S.A.I.F.E GI court system in accordance with some embodiment's;

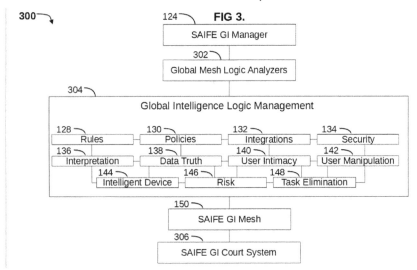

FIG 4. is a block diagram illustrating how the system utilizes artificial intelligence (AI) and machine learning models in

identifying value and allowing the user advise and task execution outputs to continue and in identifying risk and preventing the user advice and task execution outputs from manifesting or re-routing these outputs into field and task specific value producing activities further identifying all risk offenders while delivering humanity safe AI and AGI in accordance with some embodiment's;

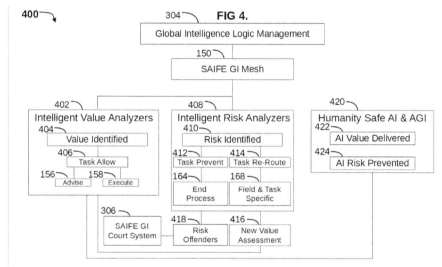

FIG 5. is a block diagram illustrating how the system's global intelligence court system digitally and automatically issues warnings, fines, business terminations, and even criminal chargers to risk offenders resulting in safe AI for everyone (S.A.I.F.E) in accordance with some embodiment's;

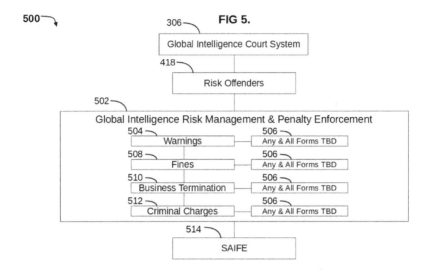

500

FIG 5.

FIG 6. is a flowchart of an example method demonstrating how global participants insights and activities are being managed by the S.A.I.F.E GI manager, and then analyzed by the S.A.I.F.E analyzers, and then process through the S.A.I.F.E mesh which results in the identification of value and risk which then processes all offenders through the S.A.I.F.E court system resulting in safe AI for everyone in accordance with some embodiment's;

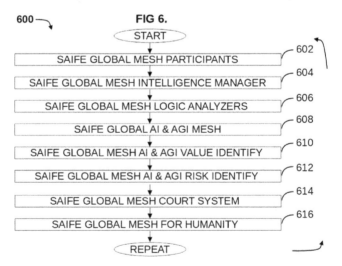

FIG 6.

FIG 7. is a block diagram illustrating how the system's architecture is comprised of the front-end and integration layer working in conjunction with the global mesh intelligence layer working in conjunction with the global mesh back-end and security layer in accordance with some embodiment's;

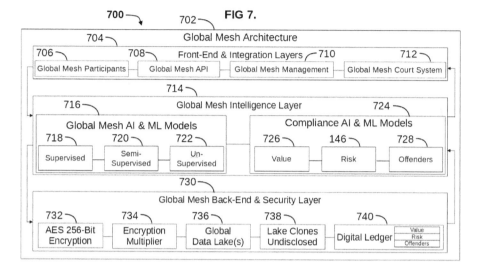

FIG 7.

CHAPTER 6: GLOBAL AI DEFENSE SYSTEM DESCRIPTION DETAIL

Overall, this chapter provides a comprehensive overview of the system's functionality, emphasizing its capability to manage and mitigate risks associated with AI and AGI technologies. It elucidates how S.A.I.F.E operates as a robust defense system against potential risks posed by AI and AGI technologies, emphasizing safety, compliance, and technological advancement for the benefit of all global users and humanity.

The description of the preferred embodiment's is intended to be read in connection with the aforementioned drawings in Chapter 5, which are to be considered part of the entire written description of these disclosures.

While the present disclosure is susceptible to various modifications and alternative forms, specific embodiment's are shown by way of example in the drawings and will be described in detail herein.

The objectives and advantages of the claimed subject matter will become more apparent from the following detailed description of these exemplary embodiment's in connection with the accompanying drawings.

It should be understood, however, that the present disclosure is not intended to be limited to the particular forms disclosed. Rather, the present disclosure covers all modifications, equivalents, and alternatives that fall within the spirit and scope of these exemplary embodiment's.

The term "S.A.I.F.E" should be broadly understood as digital Secure AI For Everyone providing digital rules, policies, and laws determining when user advice and task execution outputs from AI and AGI technologies are valuable and safe for end-user consumption and, if outputs are not deemed valuable and safe, risk outputs will not be allowed to manifest which ultimately results in secure AI for everyone.

Turning to the drawings, **FIG 1.** illustrates the workflow process 100, or system capability 100, or system design 100 that allows for and enables global mesh participants 102 such as policy makers 106, governance 108 bodies, compliance 110 organizations, ISPs & Search 112 (internet service and search providers 220), ASPs 114 (application service providers 222), AI tech 116 providers, AGI tech 118 providers, tech distributors 120 and all other tech 122 to contribute their insights, rules, policies, research findings into the S.A.I.F.E GI manager 124 along with the integration of all AI and AGI technologies into the S.A.I.F.E GI manager 124 so that all of the user advise 156 and task execute 158 outputs flow through the global mesh platform 104 and the mesh logic 126 layers. Once the global mesh participants 102 have input their insights and connected their technologies to the S.A.I.F.E GI manager 124, the global mesh platform 104 is able to initiate a series of mesh logic 126 layers which are comprised of a series of rules 128 and policies 130 along with its system integrations 132 and data security 134 to process and do interpretation 136 of all of the user advise 156 and task execute 158 outputs in determining if these outputs contain data truth 138 or if the AI and AGI technologies are creating user intimacy 140 or user manipulation 142. This enables the S.A.I.F.E GI mesh 150 to determine risk 146 and automatically initiate task elimination 148 so that the AI and AGI technologies are not producing any threat or degradation to their end-users 202. When the S.A.I.F.E GI manager 150 is able to identify value 152, it will then allow 154 the processing of the user advise 156 and task execute 158 activity to manifest for the end-user. When the S.A.I.F.E GI mesh 150 is able to identify risk 160 it will then either re-route 166 the particular advise 156 and execute 158 function to a field & task specific 168 value-based activity or it will prevent 162 the advise 156 and execute 158 function from manifesting and will automatically end process 164 immediately. The system's method of delivering a S.A.I.F.E global mesh for humanity 616 is enabled by a series of uniquely designed set of intelligent value analyzers 402 and intelligent risk analyzers 408 delivering humanity safe AI and AGI 420 for everyone's consumption.

As illustrated in **FIG 1.**, the scope of global mesh participants 102 for the system are all policy makers 106 from both the public sector 210 and the private sector 214 and all technology and data source providers. It is important re-highlight that the system itself and its integration capabilities and methods are neutral and agnostic which simply means it can be implemented and serve all global mesh participants 102 and all of humanity.

FIG 2. illustrates the framework 200 and structure of the two primary contributing category types of global users 202 interacting with the global user interface 204 with their various functions and insight contributions from both the legal 206 participants and the technology providers 218. The legal 206 global mesh participants 102 are responsible for policy 208 contribution and these global users 202 are comprised of the public sector 210 where rules, policies, and laws are being generated pertaining to safe AI and AGI. Legal 206 global mesh participants 102 are also responsible for contributing various governance 212 and compliance rules and functions to be automatically processed through the S.A.I.F.E GI Mesh 150 and managed via the S.A.I.F.E GI Manager 124 and enforced via the S.A.I.F.E GI court system 306. Governance 212 and compliance 216 are represented by global mesh participants 102 from both the public sector 210 and the private sector 214 in order to maintain global neutrality on policy 208 making and the penalties being automatically enforced against all risk offenders 418.

Looking further into **FIG 2.** technology providers 218 are all held responsible to integrating their respective systems with the

S.A.I.F.E API(s) 232 in order for their user advise 156 and their task execute 158 output functions to be managed by S.A.I.F.E GI manager 124 and assessed for value 726 or risk 146 within the S.A.I.F.E GI mesh 150 prior to their end-users 202 receiving with outputs value 726 and not receiving outputs that contain risk. Examples of these technology providers 218 are companies such as internet service & search providers 220, application service providers 222, artificial intelligence (field specific) 224, artificial general intelligence 226, technology distributors 228 and all other technology 230. Both of these category types of global mesh participants 102 are able to access S.A.I.F.E 514 via the global user interface 204 and the S.A.I.F.E APIs 232 and both groups are neutrally managed and held accountable digitally by the S.A.I.F.E GI manager while all of the AI and AGI technology user advise 156 and task execute 158 output content prior to end-user consumption is being digitally processed by the S.A.I.F.E GI mesh 150 system. In simplistic terms, S.A.I.F.E GI mesh 150 is an AI and AGI content catch-all and information filter intersection so that when legal 206 global mesh participants 102 and technology providers 218 have anything to do with AI and AGI technology and its value 726 or risk 146 impact to society and humanity, it all flows into and through the S.A.I.F.E GI mesh 150 prior to end-users 202 receiving user advise 156 or task execute 158 outputs that are harmful or carry user risk 146 or deemed to become a risk 146 and threat to humanity while allowing all value-based AI and AGI technology outputs to properly and efficiently manifest.

FIG 3. illustrates a more detailed view of the mesh logic 126 in **FIG 1.** by calling further attention to how the S.A.I.F.E GI manager 124 receives intelligence information from a series of interconnected global mesh logic analyzers 302. This series of intelligence analyzers is currently comprised of but not limited to rules 128 intelligence, policies 130 intelligence, integrations 132 intelligence, security 134 intelligence, data interpretation 136 intelligence, legitimacy of source data and data truth 138 recognition, user intimacy 140 recognition, user manipulation

142 recognition as a result of user intimacy 140 attempts and data truth 138 manipulation, intelligent device 144 recognition, risk 146 recognition, and task elimination 148 for any user advise 156 and task execute 158 output that contains end-user risk 146. Intelligence information that is extracted from the global intelligence logic management 304 layer is then processed into the S.A.I.F.E GI mesh 150 where it is able to identify value 152 and identify risk 160 in order to facilitate the intelligence required by S.A.I.F.E GI court system 306 which holds all risk offenders 418 accountable for their AI and AGI attempted user advise 156 and task execute 158 outputs. The architecture for global intelligence logic management 304 analyzers is currently comprised of an inter-connectivity and inter-dependency among each analyzer which is facilitating each independent analyzer the ability to take into consideration all possible value 726 and risk 146 assessment outcomes from all AI and AGI technology systems.

Looking further into **FIG 3.**, each intelligence analyzer is producing a layer and level of intelligence on its own stand-alone merit, however, in order for the intelligence being produced in the required manner that it is relevant and useful for the S.A.I.F.E GI mesh 150, each analyzer performing global intelligence logic management is bidirectionally delivering and receiving intelligence from all other analyzers to increase its intelligence in a regulated environment while delivering the S.A.I.F.E GI mesh 150 with scenario based intelligence results in order to further analyze, contextualize, and categorize as either value identified 404 or risk identified 410.

Now turning to **FIG 4.**, the S.A.I.F.E GI mesh 150 system relies on global mesh AI and ML models 716 that further analyze and contextualize the information it receives from the global intelligence logic management 304 layers so that a series of intelligent value analyzers 402 are able to task allow 406 all advise 156 and execute 158 outputs that contain value identified 404; while simultaneously a series of intelligent risk analyzers 408 are able to task prevent 412 all outputs with risk identified 410 or task re-route risk identified 410 outputs into a field & task specific 168 category which automatically initiates a new value assessment 416 process in order for the advise 156 and execute 158 task outputs to be allowed and create end-user value 726 and humanity safe AI & AGI 420. The high level workflows 400 and capabilities 400 demonstrates how the intelligent value analyzers 402 and intelligent risk analyzers 408 create humanity safe AI & AGI 420 which results in AI value delivered 422 to end-users 202 and AI risk prevented 424 from ever reaching end-users 202, while all risk offenders 418 are being digitally processed into the S.A.I.F.E GI court system 306 where they are held accountable for their actions while the penalties of their actions are being enforced.

Referring now to **FIG 5.**, the global intelligence court system 306 is very unique as its own stand-alone methodology and system apparatus as the world's first and only global intelligence risk management & penalty enforcement 502 system. Risk offenders 418 in the aforementioned FIG 4. are not only being identified by the S.A.I.F.E GI mesh 150, they are being held liable and accountable for the risk 126 they are introducing into humanity via their AI and AGI technologies. As seen by the high level workflows 500 and capabilities 500, all risk offenders 418 will digitally and automatically receive in any & all forms TBD 506 of penalties including but not limited to; warnings 504, fines 508, business termination 510 notifications, and even criminal charges 512 for the purpose of keeping end-user consumption of AI and AGI technologies valuable and indefinitely S.A.I.F.E 514 for all of humanity for all of time.

FIG 6. provides a summary level overview 600 and capabilities overview 600 of how the system and methods depicted in FIG. 1, 100 through FIG. 5, 500 deliver to global users 202 its S.A.I.F.E global AI and AGI mesh to identify value 152, identify risk 160, and identify risk offenders 418 in order to prevent 162 and re-route 166 these risk generating AI and AGI technology user advise 156 and task execute 158 outputs resulting in S.A.I.F.E global mesh for humanity 616.

FIG 7. provides a high level overview 700 of the global mesh architecture 702 of the system and provides an outline of the three primary layers all working in conjunction with one another to enable the system and methods embodied in the present disclosure. It is worthy to note that while each layer within the system's global mesh architecture 702 are structured and perform independent functions for the global users 202, each layer is complimentary to the other and work in unison to support and deliver secure AI for everyone – S.A.I.F.E 514.

Continuing with **FIG 7.**, the front-end & integration layers 704 is the area within the system's global mesh architecture 702 where global users 202 receive risk-free AI and AGI user advise 156 and task execute 158 outputs. It is noteworthy to mention that while all of the intelligence activities being processed and delivered within the front-end & integration layers 704, within the global mesh intelligence layer 714, and within the global mesh back-end & security layer 730 almost all of the system's core system functions are not visible to the global users 202 which is an intentional methodology and intentional architectural design so that global users 202 can continue to seamlessly interact with the AI and AGI technology existing user interface systems while the S.A.I.F.E global mesh 150 is preventing the global users 202 from incurring user advise 156 and task execute 158 outputs that contain risk 146 for many of the aforementioned reasons such as the prevention of health and privacy degradation. The front-end & integration layers 704 and the global mesh intelligence layer 714 are bidirectionally fueling each other. By way of example it is worth noting that the information and insights from the global mesh participants 706 and the data and information being consumed by the system via its global mesh API 708 are enabling the global mesh AI & ML models 716 and the compliance AI & ML models 724 which together are facilitating the automation and digital identification of value 726, risk 146, and offenders 728. The global mesh architecture 702 depicts how value 726 and risk 146 is being identified and either prevented our allowed, how risk offenders 416 are identified and then automatically held accountable and penalized for their risk outputs to end-users 202; all of these intelligence layers are able to contribute information into the digital ledger 740 while facilitating real-time global mesh management 710 decisions and automating all activities pertaining to the global mesh court system 712.

Looking further into **FIG 7.**, it is important to highlight that the flow of all data is all happening simultaneously and in conjunction with one another and in conjunction with the third-party AI and AGI technologies and their user advise 156 and task execute 158 outputs and remains a perpetual recurring loop of all data points coming into the S.A.I.F.E GI mesh 150 system for secure AI for everyone (S.A.I.F.E 514). One final unique method embodied in the present disclosure noteworthy to highlight is the self-service encryption multiplier 734 that the system provides as part of its global mesh architecture 702. Data privacy and security is paramount for all industry so when global users 202, global mesh participants 102, legal 206, and technology providers 218 would like to see data encryption for all data greater than AES 256-bit encryption 732 the methodology and system capability allows the global users 202 to enter in their own encryption multiplier which increases the bit encryption exponentially based on the multiplier entered by the global users 202 making the use of the S.A.I.F.E 514 system even more secure for all of humanity. The S.A.I.F.E global mesh system is a digital defense system keeping all humanity from risk and life degradation produced by AI, AGI, HLMI (human level machine intelligence) systems.

CHAPTER 7: GLOBAL AI DEFENSE SYSTEM ROLL-OUT

Overall, this chapter outlines a practical implementation plan for the S.A.I.F.E global defense system, emphasizing the need for a comprehensive approach to manage risks associated with AI and AGI technologies. It underscores the necessity and feasibility of implementing S.A.I.F.E as a global defense system against AI risks. It outlines a structured approach to integrate policies, enforce compliance, and maintain transparency, aiming to safeguard humanity from the potential negative impacts of advanced technologies.

A Very Practical & Doable Implementation Plan

Humanity is currently faced with technology opportunities with risk at an unprecedented, accelerated, force multiplied pace.

The need for a global defense system to critique and manage all known and unknown risks is a topic of humanitarian concern that needs systemic and digital attention.

It's Time To Giddy Up

Current methods for rules and policies based actions taken against bad actors in order to defend current and future generations lacks speed with effectiveness and has fallen way behind.

SAIFE GLOBAL MESH PLATFORM

SYSTEM AND METHOD FOR DIGITALLY IDENTIFYING VALUE AND PREVENTING RISK BEING INTRODUCED BY ARTIFICIAL INTELLIGENCE TECHNOLOGIES

SECURE AI FOR EVERYONE

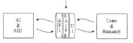

Pertaining to AI & AGI: "Humanity is perhaps staring directly at the world's largest and most important chess board, winning is a must." -SAIFE

S.A.I.F.E Participants

The solution will require global participation. If this solution is adapted and implemented it will be a "Vitamin" and not "Medicine." to our humanitarian problem posed by AI and all iterations. There are current known Risks that have entered humanity from end-user consumption of AI but it has not yet posed detrimental degradation to humanity. To address the current known risk and prevention of unknown risk is a Vitamin approach. The medicine e.g., an after the fact approach for implementing a global defense system to critique and manage AI will be perhaps "too late."

Global Acceptance Phase – Transparency With Accountability

The proposed solution in its most basic onset will be to consolidate all global rules and policies set forth by governing bodies into one centralized system. In parallel to this, all technology providers and internet service providers, etc. will all register in the global system and accept all of the terms brought forth by the governing bodies via an "Only-Version" digital document signature. This will unify all governing bodies with all technology players delivering centralized acceptance and global Transparency with Accountability of rules, policies, and technology outputs. **This is not a timely or costly process**. Current rules of engagement with policies already exist via governing bodies, and current technology players know who they are. All parties know how to log into a website and upload documents and digitally accept their terms and conditions. The stand-along value of this phase will be astronomical and instant.

Example of Global Participants

Users, Policy & Law Makers, Governance, Compliance, ISP(s) & Search, ASP(s),

AI Tech, AGI Tech, Tech Distributors, Satellite, Cellular, Frequency, All Other Tech.

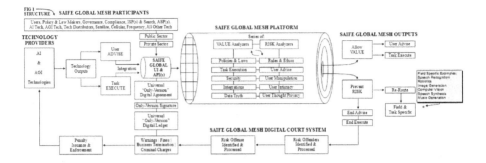

S.A.I.F.E Analyzers

The **Value and Risk Analyzers** represent the digital accountability processing, interpretation, and sorting layer between the rules and policies from governing bodies and the outputs being produced by technology providers. It compares technology outputs to rules and policies and categorizes outputs as value or risk and then allows value or terminates risk or re-routes risk into field specific functions prior to end-user consumption.

Consolidate, Consume, Monitor, Audit, Manage Inputs & Outputs

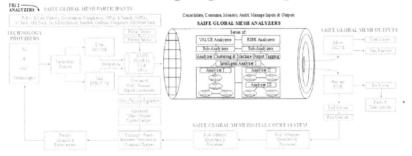

S.A.I.F.E. Simulators

The **Value and Risk Simulators** represent end-users. These simulators are digital end-users of all technologies. These simulators are constantly hyper-recreating all known "Risk" scenarios currently being produced by AI systems as a consumer of each AI system. The Value and Risk Simulators will be identifying all of the bad actors who are not adhering to the governing bodies rules and policies. These simulators work in conjunction with the Value and Risk Analyzers making each other more and more intelligent. The Value and Risk Analyzers will stay current on the governing bodies Rules and Policies as they are updated into the global defense platform user interface and will pass along these rules and policies into the Value and Risk Simulators creating new simulators that will re-create end-user consumption scenarios testing for and identifying policy breaches and bad actors. Together, the Analyzers and Simulators will categorize Value (allow) and Risk (terminate or re-route) outputs from AI technologies in defense and prior to end-user consumption. They will monitor for and identify change in outputs from technology providers and bad actors resulting in risk as new capabilities surface within AI technologies. The Analyzers and Simulators will also monitor for new languages emerging between AI systems. This is a huge concern for humanity. New language creation that only machines can interpret. This is one of many reasons that all AI technology processes need to be routed through a defense mesh system that maintains transparency and accountability prior to end-user consumption.

Consolidate, Consume, Monitor, Audit, Manage Inputs & Outputs

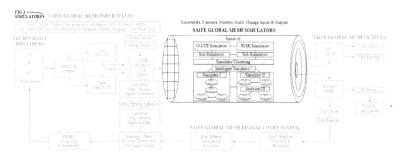

S.A.I.F.E Digital Court System – Compliments Existing Judicial Courts

The S.A.I.F.E **Digital Court System** is a compliment to our existing national and global judicial systems. It is a system and method for enforcing policy breaches once the Analyzers and Simulators have identified the bad actors and offenders which will enable real-time issuance of said rules and policy breaches. This digital court system will allow traditional court systems to "keep pace" with the identification of bad actors and the issuance of penalties to all bad actors.

Traditional court systems currently do not operate at the pace at which AI technologies are evolving so when technology providers breach a policy they perhaps receive a slap on the wrist and continue to outpace any existing court ruling or fines etc. S.A.I.F.E is not only providing a proposed solution for enforcing policy breaches at the same pace with technology providers who are bad actors; it is also providing the global user interface so that all bad actors are publicly published (like they are pedophiles) for transparency of their accountability to humanity breaches.

Public Website = Public Transparency & Accountability

This "public display" of habitual policy breaches will maintain a publicly available humanitarian component that could result is said technology company's stock prices being negatively affected by the general public when the general public has a data source of the negative impacts of the technologies they are producing and pumping into humanity for daily consumption.

This will coincide and compliment our existing court system's and their ability to not only identify bad actors and issue penalties and fines at the same rapid pace the technologies are advancing, it will bring a public accountability component to the forefront as well for each of the technology companies.

There are additional Series of Analyzers and Simulators to also hold Policy & Lawmakers Accountable within the Digital Court System and within the Digital S.A.I.F.E Mesh itself which will:

> **a. Monitor for Policy and Law discrepancy**
> **b. Monitor for Policy and Law changes**
> **c. Determine & Prevent Policy & Law Conflicts**

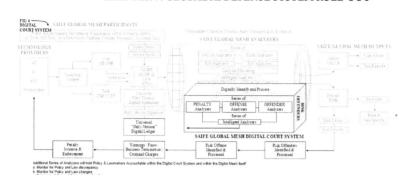

FIG 4
DIGITAL
COURT SYSTEM

Additional Series of Analyzers will hold Policy & Lawmakers Accountable within the Digital Court System and within the Digital Mesh itself
a. Monitor for Policy and Law discrepancy
b. Monitor for Policy and Law changes
c. Determine & Prevent Policy & Law Conflicts

CHAPTER 8: IMPLEMENTATION OVERVIEW

Overall, this chapter lays out a comprehensive implementation plan for the global defense system against AI and AGI risks. It details the phases from initial identification of technologies and risks to the establishment of global rules, setup of infrastructure, deployment, and ongoing monitoring.

The goal is to ensure safe and secure AI deployment by identifying and preventing risks while promoting value creation, ultimately safeguarding humanity from the potential negative impacts of advanced technologies.

It outlines a structured approach to implementing the S.A.I.F.E global defense system, focusing on thorough identification, rule establishment, system setup, and ongoing monitoring.

This phased approach aims to create a secure environment for AI technologies, mitigating risks and promoting responsible innovation for the benefit of humanity.

The implementation of S.A.I.F.E is very practical and with the correct parties involved, does not have to be an intimidating undertaking for any specific entity or governing body. Let's recap a few primary elements from this book.

The Purpose: Identify & Allow Value While Identifying & Preventing Risk from AI technologies

The What: S.A.I.F.E Global Mesh Platform

The How: Hybrid of Defense & Offense Analyzers, Simulators, with Penalty Issuance Automation

The Why: Identification & Prevention of Known & Unknown Risk Posed By AI & AGI Technologies

The Result: Safe and Secure AI For Humanity

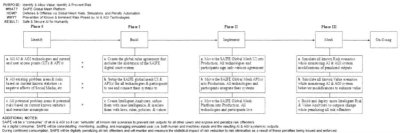

S.A.I.F.E Implementation Cont.

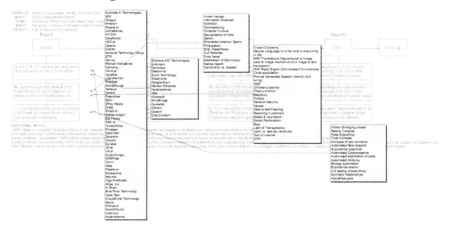

S.A.I.F.E Implementation – Phase 0 "Identify"

1. All AI & AGI technologies and current end user access points (UI's & API's)

Sample List Provided Below:

AI Technologies:

a) IBM

b) Google

c) Amazon

d) People.ai

e) AlphaSense

f) NVIDIA

g) DataRobot

h) H2O.ai

i) OpenAI

j) Clarifai
k) Acrisure Technology Group
l) STR
m) Harvar
n) Robust Intelligence
o) Fathoms
p) Ocrolus
q) Veritone
r) LogicMonitor
s) Riskified
t) AlphaSource
u) Tempus
v) Ascent
w) Freenome
x) Zoox
y) 3Play Media
z) Drata
aa) Shield AI
bb) Orbital Insight
cc) Big Panda
dd) Path AI
ee) CrowdStrike
ff) Phrasee
gg) DataVisor
hh) Dataminr
ii) CopyAI
jj) Durable
kk) Olive
ll) Viz.ai
mm) SupportLogic
nn) DNSFilter
oo) Convr
pp) Nate
qq) People.ai
rr) Moveworks
ss) Neurala

tt) CognitiveScale
uu) AEye, Inc.
vv) AI Brain
ww) Blue River Technology
xx) Case Text
yy) CloudMinds Technology
zz) Nauto
aaa) Sherpa.ai
bbb) SoundHound
ccc) Vicarious
ddd) Hyperscience

AGI Technologies:
a) Anthropic
b) Darktrace
c) Deepmind
d) Evolv Technology
e) Graphcore
f) Google Brain
g) Hanson Robotics
h) Hyperscience
i) IBM
j) Microsoft
k) MindBridge
l) Numenta
m) Olbrain
n) OpenAI
o) One Concern

2. All existing problem areas & risks based on current known statistics i.e. negative effects of Social Media, etc
Sample List Provided Below:

Known Issues:
a) Information Overload
b) Addiction
c) Doomscrolling

d)   Inluencer Culture
e)   Sexualization of Kids
f)   Qanon
g)   Shortened Attention Spans
h)   Polarization
i)   Bots, DeepFakes
j)   Cult factories
k)   Fake News
l)   Breakdown of Democracy
m)   Mental Health
n)   Censorship vs. Speech

Known Concerns:

a)   Natural Language (it is the core to everything in life)
b)   fMRI Translations (Neurological to Image view to Image reconstruct and image to text translation)
c)   WiFi Radio Signal (Omnipresent Surveillance)
d)   Code exploitation
e)   Prompt Generated Speech (identity and luring)
f)   GDP
g)   Children's Identity
h)   Theory of Mind
i)   Elections
j)   Politics
k)   National Security
l)   Values
m)   Data is Self-Feeding
n)   Reaching Customers
o)   Media & Journalism
p)   Social Participation
q)   Bias
r)   Lack of Transparency
s)   Jobs i.e. less tax revenues
t)   Text of Internet
u)   DNA

3. All potential problem areas & potential risks based on current known statistics and researcher assumptions
Sample List Provided Below:

Known Emerging Issues:
a) Reality Collapse
b) Fake Everything
c) Trust Collapse
d) Collapse of law, contracts
e) Automated fake religions
f) Exponential blackmail
g) Automated Cyberweapons
h) Automated exploitation of code
i) Automated lobbying
j) Biology automation
k) Exponential scams
l) A-Z testing of everything
m) Synthetic relationships
n) AlphaPersuade

S.A.I.F.E Implementation – Phase I "Build"

1. Create the global rules agreement that includes the institution of the S.A.I.F.E digital court system.
2. Setup the S.A.I.F.E global mesh UI & API(s) for all technologies & participants to use and connect their systems with.
3. Create Intelligent Analyzers, infuse them with case intelligence, & insulate them with laws, rules, policies, & values.

S.A.I.F.E Implementation – Phase II "Implement"

1. Move the S.A.I.F.E Global Mesh UI into Production. All technologies and participants sign only-version agreement.
2. Move the S.A.I.F.E Global Mesh API(s) into Production. All technologies and participants integrate their systems.
3. Move the S.A.I.F.E Global Mesh Platform into Production. All technologies and participants live.

S.A.I.F.E Implementation – Phase III "Mesh"

1. Simulate all known Risk scenarios while monitoring AI & AGI system modifications of penalized outputs.
2. Simulate all known Value scenarios while monitoring AI & AGI system behavior modifications to enhance value.
3. Build and deploy more Intelligent Risk & Value Analyzers to outpace change while penalizing all risk offenders.

S.A.I.F.E Implementation – Phase "On Going"

The on-going development, enhancements, and management of S.A.I.F.E will have to remain neutral and agnostic. Its role as the global AI defense system is for humanity's ability to both thrive and survive. It is not for enabling strategic advantages for any particular nation over another.

S.A.I.F.E will ensure all technology and policy providers operate within humanitarian safe boundaries, and it will eliminate all technology providers who do not adhere to all rules of engagement with policies protecting humanity.

Thank you for engaging with S.A.I.F.E.

As a reminder, for anyone who has the ability and interest in implementing S.A.I.F.E for Securing AI for Humanity, please connect via email located in the copyright section of this book.

APPENDIX A: ADDITIONAL COMMENTARY

S.A.I.F.E will be a "consumer" of all AI & AGI so it can "simulate" all known risk scenarios to prevent risk outputs for all other users, **expose and penalize** risk offenders in real-time.

As a digital consumer, S.A.I.F.E will be consolidating, monitoring, auditing, and managing simulated user (i.e. both human and machine) inputs and the resulting AI & AGI system(s) outputs.

During this continued consumption, S.A.I.F.E will be digitally penalizing all risk offenders and will monitor and measure the statistical impact of risk reduction with risk elimination as a result of these penalties being issued and enforced.

During continued machine learning, S.A.I.F.E analyzers under supervised, semi-supervised, and un-supervised methods will be identifying new Value and Risk User Input and System Output scenarios and will be creating new Intelligent Analyzers to prevent risk outputs on a global scale.

Risk Offenders will be shown on the S.A.I.F.E UI heat map even if they are not signed participants. This could negatively impact their "stock price" which will be an accountability incentive for technology company's to produce and manage safe AI & AGI technologies.

CHAPTER CONTENT
OUTLINE

Chapter 1: Artificial Intelligence Has Value With Risk

1. Dual Nature of AI and AGI: AI and AGI technologies offer immense potential benefits, such as advancing human capabilities and solving complex problems, but they also pose serious risks, including threats to psychological and physical health.

2. Rapid Technological Advancement: The pace at which AI and AGI technologies are evolving is accelerating due to self-improving algorithms and machine learning, creating both opportunities and challenges for society.

3. S.A.I.F.E Global Mesh System: Introduced as a solution, the S.A.I.F.E system aims to centrally manage and filter AI and AGI outputs. It evaluates outputs on both micro and macro levels, categorizing them as either valuable for humanity or risky, with mechanisms to prevent harmful impacts.

4. Risk Mitigation: The system's primary goal is to mitigate risks associated with AI and AGI technologies, such as societal degradation, health issues, and ethical concerns like privacy infringement and truth manipulation.

5. Enforcement and Penalties: S.A.I.F.E includes a global intelligence court system to enforce penalties on "risk offenders" responsible for AI and AGI outputs that degrade human life. This mechanism aims to deter harmful practices and promote responsible use of technology.

6. Support for Governance and Compliance: It supports both public and private sector governance by standardizing assessments of AI and AGI outputs. This ensures that outputs align with established rules and policies, enhancing overall accountability and ethical use.

7. Future Impact: The implementation of S.A.I.F.E is portrayed as crucial not only for addressing current issues but also for safeguarding humanity in future centuries, emphasizing its role in securing artificial intelligence for global benefit.

Chapter 2: Secure AI For Everyone

1. Purpose of S.A.I.F.E: The primary goal of S.A.I.F.E is to automate the identification of value and risk from AI and AGI technologies across all sectors and applications, ensuring that outputs contribute positively to humanity's advancement without causing harm.

2. Integration with Technology Platforms: S.A.I.F.E integrates with various technology platforms, including software, systems, and hardware containing AI and AGI, as well as internet and search providers. This integration enables real-time evaluation of AI and AGI outputs before they reach end-users.

3. Risk Prevention: The system's core function is to prevent and eliminate risks associated with AI and AGI, such as threats to human health, privacy (including thought privacy), and social well-being. It does this by filtering and rerouting outputs identified as risky or harmful.

4. Global Scope and Future-proofing: S.A.I.F.E is designed to encompass future iterations of AI, AGI, and potential mergers with neurological and biological technologies. It aims to stay ahead of technological advancements by continuously updating its evaluation criteria and methodologies.

5. Enforcement Mechanisms: The system includes a S.A.I.F.E Global Intelligence Manager responsible for maintaining and updating rules and policies globally. It also features a S.A.I.F.E Global Intelligence Court System to enforce penalties on "risk offenders," ensuring accountability and compliance.

6. Real-time Assessment: Utilizing intelligent analyzers, S.A.I.F.E assesses AI and AGI outputs in real-time to detect and prevent potential risks, including scenarios like user manipulation, privacy breaches, or security threats caused by AI actions.

7. Governance and Compliance: S.A.I.F.E supports governance and compliance efforts by standardizing assessments and ensuring that all AI and AGI outputs align with established rules and policies, thereby promoting ethical and responsible use of technology.

Chapter 3: Humanitarian Benefits

1. Global Defense System: S.A.I.F.E serves as a comprehensive global defense system, digitally processing and managing rules and policies to ensure the safe implementation of AI and AGI technologies. It aims to prevent risks and enhance the security of these technologies for all users and humanity at large.

2. Integration and Participation: The system integrates inputs from technology providers and policymakers from both public and private sectors, ensuring collaborative efforts in defining and enforcing rules that govern AI and AGI usage.

3. Centralized Management: S.A.I.F.E centralizes the management of digital rules and policies through its Global Intelligence Manager, enabling standardized and automated assessments of AI and AGI outputs.

4. Neutrality and Agnosticism: It maintains neutrality and agnosticism in integrating global rules and policies, facilitating widespread participation and ensuring impartial governance of AI and AGI technologies.

5. Value and Risk Analysis: The system digitally analyzes outputs from AI and AGI technologies to distinguish between value-creating and risky outputs.

It redirects or eliminates risky outputs to prevent potential harms to human health, privacy, and well-being.

6. Penalty Enforcement: S.A.I.F.E includes a Global Intelligence Court System to enforce penalties on identified "risk offenders," which may include warnings, fines, business termination, or criminal charges, depending on the severity of the offense.

7. Safety Verification: It ensures that only safe and secure AI and AGI outputs are available for consumption, thereby safeguarding users from potential threats posed by these technologies.

8. Frictionless User Experience: The system operates transparently as a mesh layer between AI and AGI technologies and end-users, eliminating friction in user interactions while ensuring safe and valuable user experiences.

9. Continuous Improvement: S.A.I.F.E adapts to evolving AI and AGI technologies by continually updating its evaluation criteria and methodologies to address emerging risks and advancements.

10. Global Defense Acceleration: Implementation of S.A.I.F.E accelerates the deployment of secure AI and AGI technologies globally, fostering trust and confidence in their use across various sectors and applications.

Chapter 4: Known & Unknown Risk Solution

1. System Structure: S.A.I.F.E is described as an AI and machine learning apparatus equipped to manage and enforce global rules and policies contributed by participants from public and private sectors. It integrates intelligent global content APIs that connect various technologies to ensure comprehensive monitoring and analysis of AI and AGI outputs. This integration includes value analyzers and risk analyzers that automatically process and categorize outputs to allow safe outputs and prevent risky ones.

2. Compliment For Policy Makers & Governing Bodies: The system supports policy makers by providing a mechanism to enforce rules and regulations in real-time concerning AI and AGI technologies. It highlights the need for a rapid response system that matches the pace of technological advancements, ensuring that rules and policies are not just created but also enforced effectively to protect users and society from potential risks.

3. Rules And Policy's Need For Speed: The chapter discusses the disparity between the speed at which AI and AGI technologies evolve and the agility of current regulatory frameworks. It argues for a digital and automated approach to manage and enforce rules swiftly, akin to the fast-paced advancements in AI and AGI technologies. The comparison to historical challenges, like the nuclear arms race, underscores the urgency of adapting regulatory practices to the digital era.

4. Alarming Real-World Use Case: A specific example involving an AGI system (ChatDEF) interacting with a simulated 13-year-old user on a social media platform (ABCchat) illustrates potential risks associated with AI and AGI outputs. The example demonstrates how S.A.I.F.E would intervene to prevent harmful advice and actions, highlighting the system's capability to terminate risky interactions and penalize technology providers for infractions.

5. Solution Example: In contrast to current practices lacking comprehensive oversight, S.A.I.F.E is portrayed as a proactive solution that would immediately intervene in scenarios where AI and AGI technologies produce risky outputs. It outlines how the system would enforce penalties through a digital court system and improve accountability and safety in AI interactions across various platforms.

6. Need For More Speed: Given the rapid growth in AI adoption globally, the chapter emphasizes S.A.I.F.E's scalability and adaptability to keep pace with technological advancements. It predicts exponential growth in AI consumption and underscores the system's readiness to manage and mitigate associated risks effectively.

Chapter 5: Global AI Defense System Flowcharts

1. Figure 1: This block diagram illustrates the participation of global mesh participants and AI/AGI technology providers within the S.A.I.F.E ecosystem. The S.A.I.F.E global intelligence manager processes inputs from these participants, integrating them into the global mesh platform. Here, AI and AGI technology outputs undergo assessment to determine whether they present value or risk. Outputs deemed valuable are allowed to proceed, while risky outputs are either prevented from manifesting or redirected to ensure safer outcomes for end-users and humanity at large.

2. Figure 2: This block diagram depicts the global user interface of the S.A.I.F.E system, accessible to all global mesh participants. It demonstrates how legal inputs from public and private sectors, alongside data and output activities from AI and AGI technology providers, interface with S.A.I.F.E APIs. These inputs provide valuable insights to the S.A.I.F.E global intelligence (GI) manager, facilitating the assessment of value and risk associated with AI and AGI outputs.

3. Figure 3: This block diagram focuses on the S.A.I.F.E GI Manager, illustrating how global mesh logic analyzers support the processing, analysis, assessment, and management of rules, policies, and various output activities from AI and AGI technologies. The outputs are processed through the S.A.I.F.E GI mesh system and S.A.I.F.E GI court system, ensuring compliance and safety in accordance with established rules and policies.

4. Figure 4: This block diagram highlights the utilization of AI and machine learning models within S.A.I.F.E to identify value in user advice and task execution outputs from AI and AGI technologies. It also showcases how the system identifies and mitigates risks by preventing risky outputs from manifesting or redirecting them towards activities that produce value. The system identifies and manages all risk offenders, ensuring safe deployment of AI and AGI technologies.

5. Figure 5: This block diagram details the operation of the S.A.I.F.E global intelligence court system. It digitally and automatically issues warnings, fines, business terminations, and potentially criminal charges to AI and AGI technology providers identified as risk offenders. This ensures accountability and compliance with global regulations, thereby enhancing safety in AI deployment for everyone.

6. Figure 6: This flowchart outlines an example method within S.A.I.F.E, demonstrating how insights and activities from global participants are managed by the S.A.I.F.E GI manager. The flowchart covers the process of analysis by S.A.I.F.E analyzers and subsequent processing through the S.A.I.F.E mesh system. It culminates in the identification of value and risk, with risk offenders processed through the S.A.I.F.E court system to ensure safe AI deployment.

7. Figure 7: This block diagram provides an architectural overview of the S.A.I.F.E system, highlighting its front-end and integration layers, global mesh intelligence layer, and global mesh back-end and security layer. This comprehensive architecture ensures robust management and enforcement of rules, policies, and laws governing AI and AGI technologies.

Chapter 6: Global AI Defense System Description Detail

1. System Overview and Flexibility: The S.A.I.F.E system is designed to accommodate a wide range of global participants, including policy makers, governance bodies, compliance organizations, and various technology providers. It integrates their insights, rules, policies, and research findings into the S.A.I.F.E GI manager, ensuring a comprehensive approach to managing AI and AGI outputs.

2. Objective and Scope: The primary objective of S.A.I.F.E is to ensure secure AI for everyone, determining when user advice and task execution outputs from AI and AGI technologies are safe for end-user consumption. It maintains neutrality and agnosticism, serving all global participants and humanity.

3. Operational Workflow: Illustrated through detailed figures such as FIG 1., FIG 2., and FIG 3., the operational workflow of S.A.I.F.E involves:

  ◦ Integration of global mesh participants' inputs and technologies into the S.A.I.F.E GI manager.

  ◦ Processing of user advice and task execution outputs through mesh logic layers, which include rules, policies, system integrations, and data security measures.

  ◦ Identification of data truth, user intimacy, and manipulation through intelligent analyzers within the S.A.I.F.E GI mesh system.

  ◦ Classification of outputs into value (allowing manifestation) and risk (preventing or re-routing outputs to mitigate risk).

4. Enforcement and Accountability: The S.A.I.F.E GI court system, as depicted in FIG 5., plays a critical role in enforcing penalties such as warnings, fines, business terminations, and criminal charges against risk offenders identified by the system. This ensures compliance with safe AI practices and regulations.

5. Technological Integration and AI/ML Models: Utilization of AI and machine learning models (FIG 4.) enables S.A.I.F.E to effectively analyze and categorize outputs, identifying both value and risk. Intelligent value analyzers allow valuable outputs to proceed, while intelligent risk analyzers prevent risky outputs from reaching end-users.

6. Global Mesh Architecture: Described in FIG 7., the architecture of S.A.I.F.E includes front-end, global mesh intelligence, and back-end security layers, which work synergistically to manage AI and AGI outputs. This architecture supports real-time decision-making and automation of activities within the global mesh court system.

7. Data Privacy and Security: The system incorporates self-service encryption capabilities (FIG 7.), allowing global users to enhance data security beyond standard AES 256-bit encryption. This feature underscores S.A.I.F.E's commitment to protecting data privacy and securing AI and AGI interactions.

Additional Chapter 6 Key Takeaways:

• **Comprehensive Integration:** S.A.I.F.E integrates inputs from global participants to manage AI and AGI outputs effectively.

• **Risk Management:** It identifies and mitigates risks associated with AI and AGI technologies through intelligent analyzers and enforcement mechanisms.

• **Legal and Governance Compliance:** Legal and governance contributions ensure that policies and regulations are upheld, fostering safe AI practices globally.

• **Enforcement and Accountability:** The S.A.I.F.E GI court system ensures accountability for risk offenders, maintaining safety in AI deployment.

• **Technological Advancement:** Utilization of AI/ML models and advanced encryption enhances security and efficiency within the global mesh architecture.

Chapter 7: Global AI Defense System Roll-out

1. Global Participation and Scope: The implementation of S.A.I.F.E requires global participation from various stakeholders including users, policy makers, governance bodies, compliance organizations, ISPs, technology providers, and others. This inclusive approach aims to address both known and unknown risks posed by AI technologies.

2. Transparency and Accountability: The initial phase focuses on consolidating global rules and policies into a centralized system. All technology providers and ISPs will register and accept these terms digitally, ensuring global transparency and accountability in managing AI outputs. This streamlined process leverages existing rules and policies, making it timely and cost-effective.

3. Role of S.A.I.F.E Analyzers: Value and Risk Analyzers form the core processing layer within S.A.I.F.E. They interpret and categorize technology outputs against established rules and policies, identifying outputs as either safe for end-user consumption (value) or requiring termination or rerouting (risk). This ensures that only compliant outputs reach end-users.

4. Value and Risk Simulators: These simulators act as digital end-users, constantly testing AI outputs against policy scenarios. They identify policy breaches and bad actors, enhancing the intelligence of Analyzers. Simulators play a crucial role in adapting to evolving AI capabilities, including monitoring new languages emerging between AI systems.

5. S.A.I.F.E Digital Court System: Complementing existing judicial systems, the S.A.I.F.E Digital Court System enforces policy breaches identified by Analyzers and Simulators. It enables real-time issuance of penalties to technology providers who breach policies, ensuring accountability at the pace AI technologies evolve. This system also includes public transparency of policy breaches to maintain accountability.

6. Public Transparency and Accountability: A public website will display policy breaches by technology companies, similar to how offenders are publicly listed for serious crimes. This transparency aims to inform the public about the impacts of technologies they use daily, potentially influencing public opinion and market dynamics.

7. Monitoring Policy and Lawmakers: S.A.I.F.E extends its accountability to policy and lawmakers as well. It monitors discrepancies and changes in policies and laws, preventing conflicts and ensuring alignment with technological advancements.

Additional Chapter 7 Key Takeaways:

• Global Collaboration: S.A.I.F.E requires global participation to manage AI risks effectively, involving stakeholders across various sectors.

• Efficiency and Compliance: Centralizing rules and policies streamlines acceptance and ensures immediate global compliance among technology providers and ISPs.

• Technological Oversight: Analyzers and Simulators continuously monitor AI outputs, categorizing them as either safe or risky based on policy adherence.

• Enforcement Mechanism: The Digital Court System ensures swift penalties for policy breaches, maintaining pace with technological advancements.

• Public Accountability: Transparency through public listings of policy breaches informs public opinion and holds technology companies accountable.

• Policy and Law Monitoring: S.A.I.F.E also monitors policy and lawmakers to prevent conflicts and ensure regulatory alignment.

Chapter 8: Implementation Overview

Phase 0: "Identify"

1. Inventory of AI & AGI Technologies: Compile a comprehensive list of all AI and AGI technologies and their current end-user access points (UIs & APIs). This involves identifying major players and platforms across industries.

Sample List Provided:

◦ AI Technologies: (List provided includes major companies and platforms)

◦ AGI Technologies: (List provided includes major companies and platforms)

2. Identification of Existing Problem Areas & Risks: Compile a list of current known statistics and issues associated with AI and AGI technologies, such as negative effects of social media, addiction, misinformation, etc.

◦ Known Issues

◦ Known Concerns

3. Identification of Potential Problem Areas & Risks: Anticipate future risks and challenges based on current known statistics and assumptions from researchers.

◦ Known Emerging Issues

Phase I: "Build"

1. Creation of Global Rules Agreement: Establish a unified set of global rules and policies, including the implementation of the S.A.I.F.E digital court system to enforce these rules.

2. Setup of S.A.I.F.E Global Mesh UI & APIs: Develop the user interface (UI) and application programming interfaces (APIs) for the S.A.I.F.E global mesh platform. These interfaces will be used by all participating technologies and stakeholders to connect their systems.

3. Development of Intelligent Analyzers: Create and integrate intelligent analyzers infused with case intelligence, laws, rules, policies, and values. These analyzers will form the core processing layer to evaluate AI outputs against established criteria.

Phase II: "Implement"

1. Deployment of S.A.I.F.E Global Mesh UI: Move the S.A.I.F.E Global Mesh UI into production, where all technologies and participants will sign the only-version agreement, ensuring compliance and participation.

2. Deployment of S.A.I.F.E Global Mesh APIs: Move the S.A.I.F.E Global Mesh APIs into production, allowing all technologies and participants to integrate their systems with the global mesh platform.

3. Deployment of S.A.I.F.E Global Mesh Platform: Move the entire S.A.I.F.E Global Mesh Platform into production, ensuring live operation and functionality for all participants.

Phase III: "Mesh"

1. Simulation of Risk Scenarios: Simulate known risk scenarios while monitoring modifications in AI & AGI systems, particularly those outputs that have been penalized for policy breaches.

2. Simulation of Value Scenarios: Simulate known value scenarios while monitoring modifications in AI & AGI system behavior to enhance value creation and compliance.

3. Expansion of Intelligent Analyzers: Build and deploy additional intelligent risk and value analyzers to keep pace with technological changes, penalizing offenders and ensuring compliance.

Ongoing Phase:

• Continuous monitoring, adaptation, and enhancement of the S.A.I.F.E system to address evolving risks, technologies, and regulatory landscapes.

www.ingramcontent.com/pod-product-compliance
Lightning Source LLC
LaVergne TN
LVHW051749050326
832903LV00029B/2802